Ukrainian Egg Decoration:
A Holiday Tradition

Ann Stalcup

The Rosen Publishing Group's
PowerKids Press™
New York

To my husband, Ed, who shares my love of folk art and travel

Special thanks to Marta Baczynsky and Chrystyna Pevny at the Ukrainian Museum, New York, for their help and generosity.

Published in 1999 by The Rosen Publishing Group, Inc.
29 East 21st Street, New York, NY 10010

First Edition

Book Design: Resa Listort

Photo Credits: p. 4 © Natalie Fobes/Corbis; pp. 6, 7, 9, 19 © Jim Sugar Photography/Corbis; p. 8 © Hulton-Deutsch/Corbis; p. 11 © Outland, Joe/Corbis; p. 12 © Keren Sue/Corbis; p. 15 © Martha Cooper/Viesti; p. 16 © Reuters/Mikhail Chernickin/Archive Photos; pp. 20, 21 by Christine Innamorato.

Stalcup, Ann, 1935-
     Ukrainian egg decoration : A holiday tradition / by Ann Stalcup.
          p.   cm. — (Crafts of the world)
     Includes index.
     Summary: Describes *pysanky,* the traditional folk craft of decorating Easter eggs as carried on by women in Ukraine, a country on the northern edge of the Black Sea.
     ISBN 0-8239-5335-1
     1. Egg decoration—Ukraine—Juvenile literature. 2. Easter eggs—Ukraine—Juvenile literature. [1. Egg decoration—Ukraine. 2. Easter eggs—Ukraine. 3. Handicraft. 4. Ukraine—Social life and customs.] I. Title. II. Series: Crafts of the world (New York, N.Y.)
     TT896.7.S73 1998
     745.594'4—dc21   98-16291
                                                                                                                               CIP
                                                                                                                               AC

Manufactured in the United States of America

Contents

What Are *Pysanky?*

Pysanky (pih-SAHN-kee) are beautifully decorated eggs. Decorating *pysanky* is a **tradition** (truh-DIH-shun) that comes from the country of Ukraine. Ukraine is on the eastern edge of Europe. The word *pysanky* comes from the Ukrainian word *pysaty*, which means to write. It is believed that this form of egg decoration started around 4,000 BC.

To make *pysanky*, beautiful **designs** (dih-ZYNZ) are drawn on eggs with a special tool that has been dipped in **beeswax** (BEEZ-waks). This tradition has been passed down from mother to daughter for thousands of years.

Pysanky are made before the Christian holiday of Easter. They **represent** (reh-pree-ZENT) spring and **rebirth** (REE-berth).

◀ The tradition of creating *pysanky* is still very much alive today.

Writing with Wax

A tool called a **kistka** (KIST-kuh) is used to write on the eggs with melted beeswax. A *kistka* is like a pen that uses wax instead of ink.

The decorator draws a design on an egg with melted wax and then dips the egg into a light-color dye, such as yellow. The egg will stay white wherever the wax was written. When the egg is dry, another wax design is written on the egg. The egg is then dropped into a darker-color dye, such as orange. Wherever the wax is written in this step, the egg will stay yellow. This is repeated over and over again with dyes of different colors. The darkest colors are saved for last. The wax is removed by holding the egg next to a candle flame.

It takes many years of practice to design and dye beautiful *pysanky*. ▶

6

Decorating in Secret

Ukrainian women are very proud of their *pysanky*. No woman wants her ideas copied, so people sometimes decorate their eggs in private. No two eggs are ever exactly alike. Often the eggs aren't seen by anyone until they are blessed in church on Easter Sunday.

The eggs that are decorated are not cooked. If the uncooked *pysanky* are left in a cool, open area, the inside of the egg will slowly dry up. *Pysanky* can last for a very long time.

◀ Women have been gathering to create *pysanky* for many years.

Pysanky Legends

Some Ukrainians believe in a very old **legend** (LEH-jend) that says the **fate** (FAYT) of the world depends on the creation of *pysanky*. Many Ukrainians believe that *pysanky* keep evil away from people and families. The more *pysanky* that are created before Easter, the harder it is for evil to get stronger. But if only a few *pysanky* are made, or none at all, then evil will be very strong. If this were to happen, people believe that bad things would happen all over the world.

This is one of the reasons that *pysanky* are created every spring.

Pysanky are created every year because of tradition, and also because they are beautiful and fun to make. ▶

Krashanky

Krashanky (kruh-SHAN-kee) comes from a Russian word meaning color. *Krashanky* eggs are another important Easter tradition. Unlike *pysanky*, you can eat *krashanky*. *Krashanky* eggs are hard-boiled and dyed one bright color.

Many people who **celebrate** (SEL-uh-brayt) Easter **fast** (FAST) for part of the 40 days and nights before Easter. This time is called Lent. Instead of giving up food completely during Lent, many families eat small amounts of plain food. On Easter Sunday, the fast is broken by eating *krashanky*.

◀ *Krashanky* are usually the only Ukrainian Easter eggs that are cooked.

Easter Traditions

On Easter Sunday, families bring Easter baskets to church to be blessed. In each basket are *pysanky* and *krashanky*, bread called *paska*, and some meat. The priest blesses the baskets, and, after mass, families return home. At home, the father takes the *krashanky* and cracks it open. He cuts the egg into pieces, and the whole family eats part of it. This ends the fast.

The gift of a decorated egg **symbolizes** (SIM-buh-ly-zez) friendship, love, and peace. The women **admire** (ad-MYR) one another's eggs, and together they celebrate the arrival of spring.

Families look forward to the blessing of their Easter baskets on Easter Sunday. ▶

Pysanky and the Sun

Farming has always been important to Ukrainian people. In fact, much of Ukrainian life is tied to nature and the land. The sun is needed for the growth of crops. In Ukrainian tradition, the egg is considered a **symbol** (SIM-bul) of the sun. *Pysanky* are very special because they celebrate the importance of the sun.

Pysanky eggs are always made in the spring. This is when the sun melts the winter's snow, and flowers, trees, and crops begin to grow again.

◀ A large amount of wheat grows in Ukraine every year. Because of this, Ukraine is often called "the bread basket of Eastern Europe."

Design Symbols

Some people believe that *pysanky* have special powers. Different symbols are written on the eggs to show these powers. Each symbol has a meaning, but the meaning may change from village to village. For example, dots symbolize stars, butterflies symbolize nature, and birds symbolize happiness and spring. Flowers symbolize love, animals symbolize **prosperity** (prah-SPEHR-ih-tee), and wheat symbolizes health and a good **harvest** (HAR-vist). Roosters symbolize wishes coming true, and patterns that circle the egg symbolize **eternal** (ih-TER-nul) life.

The symbol of the rooster is very common because roosters announce when the sun is rising. ▶

Egg Dying

You will need:

one or two hard-boiled eggs
a sharpened white crayon
water
food coloring
white vinegar
empty egg carton
    (to use as a drying rack)
toothpick
paper
pencil

1. Practice some designs on paper before you design your egg.

2. Draw your design on the egg with white crayon.

3. You can scratch smaller designs into the white crayon marks with a toothpick.

4. Mix a few drops of food coloring and 2 teaspoons of vinegar in 1 cup of water.

5. Gently place the egg in the dye and let it soak. The longer you let it soak, the brighter the color will be.

6. You can wait for your dyed egg to dry and then dip it into another color. Or you can dip half the egg in one color, and half the egg in another color. Be creative!

7. Let the egg dry.

Pysanky Traditions in North America

Many Ukrainians now live in the United States and Canada. They have brought with them their tradition of *pysanky* decoration. Each spring Ukrainian women and girls continue to decorate eggs just like their great-grandmothers did in the past. In some areas of Canada there are contests each spring for the best eggs.

Pysanky will bring good luck to families. The beliefs connected with these beautiful eggs are still very much a part of Ukrainian lives and **heritage** (HEHR-ih-tij). And around the world people of all ages are keeping the tradition of Ukrainian egg decoration alive.

Glossary

admire (ad-MYR) To respect, or like very much.

beeswax (BEEZ-waks) Wax that is made by bees.

celebrate (SEL-uh-brayt) To enjoy a special time in honor of someone or something.

design (dih-ZYN) A pattern that decorates something, such as an egg.

eternal (ih-TER-nul) Lasting forever.

fast (FAST) To eat very little or nothing at all.

fate (FAYT) The power that supposedly decides what will happen in the future.

harvest (HAR-vist) A season's gathered crop.

heritage (HEHR-ih-tij) The cultural traditions that are handed down from parent to child.

kistka (KIST-kuh) The tool used to write with melted wax.

krashanky (kruh-SHAN-kee) Hard-boiled eggs that are dyed one bright color.

legend (LEH-jend) A story passed down through the years that many people believe.

prosperity (prah-SPEHR-ih-tee) To do well.

pysanky (pih-SAHN-kee) Eggs that are decorated using wax and dyes in the Ukrainian tradition.

rebirth (REE-berth) To be born again.

represent (reh-pree-ZENT) To stand for something else.

symbol (SIM-bul) An object or design that stands for something important.

symbolize (SIM-buh-lyz) To stand for something important.

tradition (truh-DIH-shun) A belief or custom handed down from the past.

Index